THIS BRIDGE WILL NOT BE GRAY

THIS BRIDGE WILL NOT BE GRAY

STORY BY
DAVE EGGERS

ART BY
TUCKER NICHOLS

McSWEENEY'S

In the beginning there was a bridge.

No, before that, there was a bay.
A bay that led to the ocean.
This ocean was the Pacific.

THE MIGHTY
PACIFIC

The passageway between the bay and the ocean was called the Golden Gate. On one side of the Golden Gate was the Presidio, a military base at the top of the city of San Francisco. On the other side there were only hills, green and yellow, rising high above the sea. Beyond these hills were a series of small towns along the coast.

The only way to get to these towns was by boat, or by going very far north and coming back down again. It was not easy.

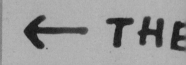

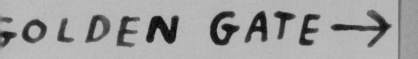

So over the years many had proposed building a bridge
between San Francisco and these hills.

But many more thought this a very bad idea.
It will mar the beauty of this land, they said.

What's wrong with boats? they said.

But this book is not about the debate to build the bridge. This book is about the shape and color of the bridge they did build.

In 1928 it was decided to build a bridge, and a man named Joseph Strauss was hired to design it. Originally from Cincinnati, Joseph was an expert in all kinds of bridges.

The first design he came up with was the strangest, most awkward and plain old ugly bridge anyone had ever seen. This is actually what it looked like.

People compared it to an upside-down rat trap. They thought he'd lost his mind.

But he had not lost his mind. He was a scientific man, and he had designed a scientific bridge. It was functional, but it was grotesque.

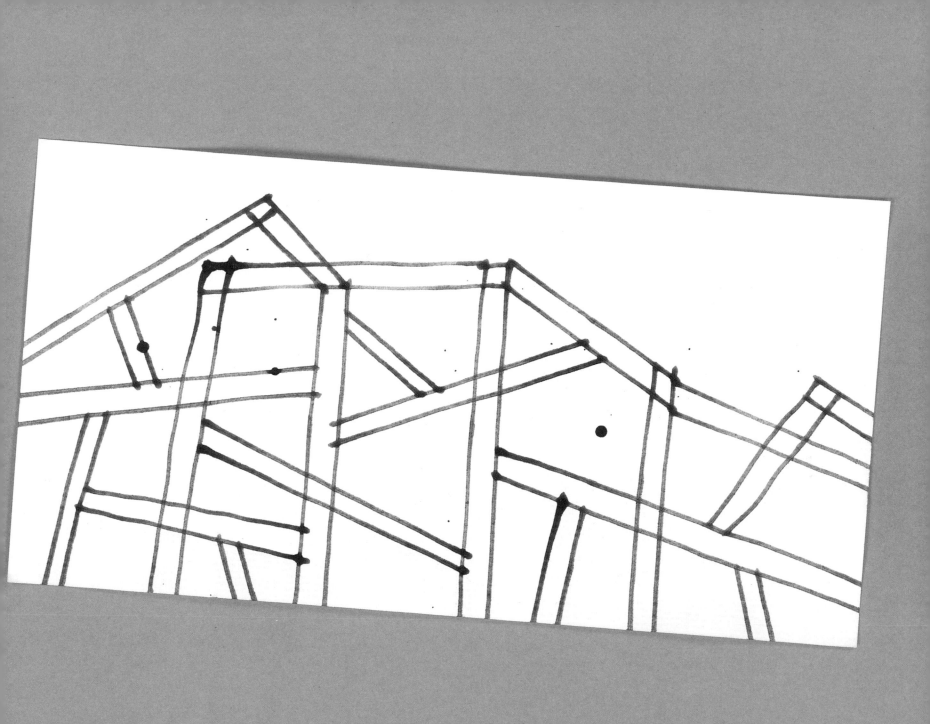

Functional but ugly, the people said, wasn't good enough. This bridge, built to span this beautiful land against this beautiful sea, had to be beautiful itself.

So he tried again.
This time he asked
for help.

One of his helpers
was Leon Moisseiff.
Leon had come to the
USA from Latvia and
had become one of
the most respected
bridge designers in the
world. He designed
the Manhattan Bridge,
which is believed to be
in or near New York City.

Leon designed a suspension bridge,
one with swooping lines and tall towers.
It would be the longest suspension bridge
in the world. It would be the tallest, too.

Everyone was excited
about this design.

I like it very much,
said this man.

My aunt likes it very much,
said this woman.

This third person was chewing food but seemed to agree with the other two people.

But still the bridge appeared a bit stern in style. So Joseph and Leon asked another person, named Irving Morrow, to help out.

Irving Morrow was an architect, and his wife, Gertrude, was an architect, too, and together they lived not far from the Golden Gate. They designed homes, and gardens, but Irving had never designed anything at all like a bridge. Nothing this big or grand or important to so many people all at once.

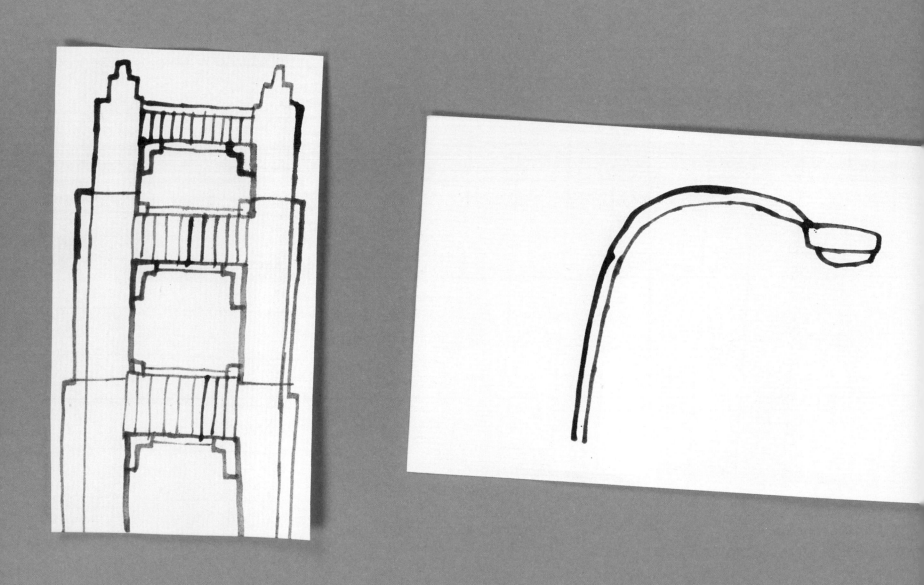

Irving threw himself into the work. He suggested that the bridge have vertical fluting and art deco flourishes. He suggested pedestrian walkways on either side of the bridge. He suggested that there be beautiful lamps along the walkways. Just about none of these things was necessary for the functioning of the bridge—they could have just built it plainer, and cheaper, and quicker—but Irving Morrow thought that the bridge could be both a bridge and something like art. This was a new idea to many of the people who were involved in this project.

So eventually the bridge was designed, and steelworkers in Maryland, Pennsylvania, and New Jersey began building the bridge, piece by piece, in thousands of sections. These sections were put on railcars, and then on boats, and these boats took these parts all the way down the coast of North America, through the Panama Canal, and up the coast of Mexico and California.

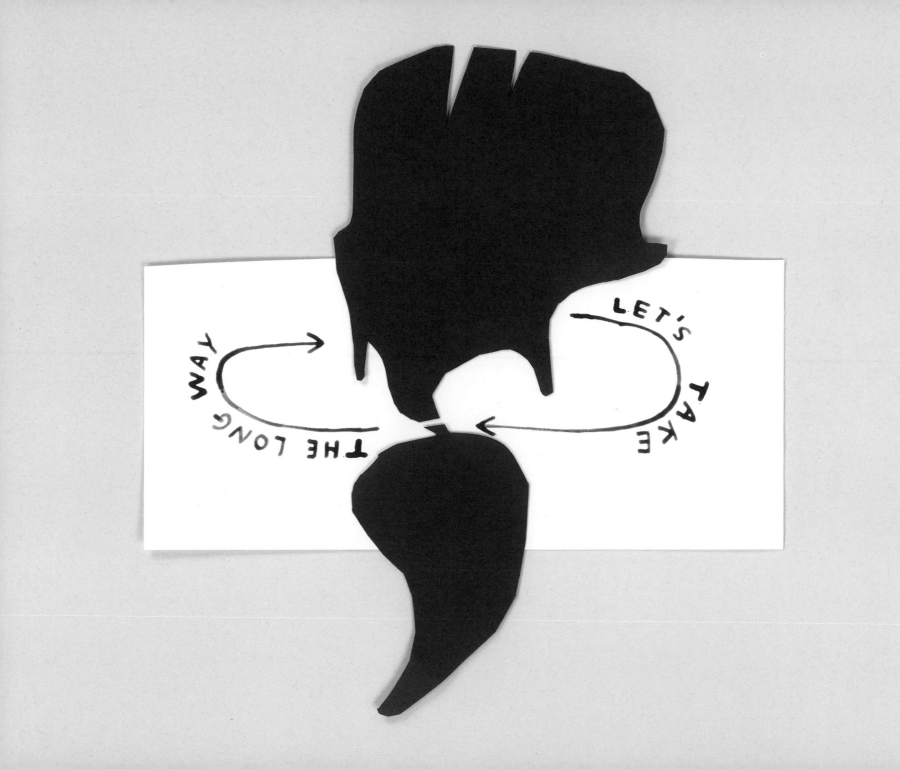

It was a long trip, but the pieces of steel did not
mind, for they are inanimate objects.

Finally it was time to construct the bridge. Men had to dive into the freezing ocean to sink the bridge's foundation. Other men, sitting high above the ocean, connected the parts. It was dangerous and complicated work.

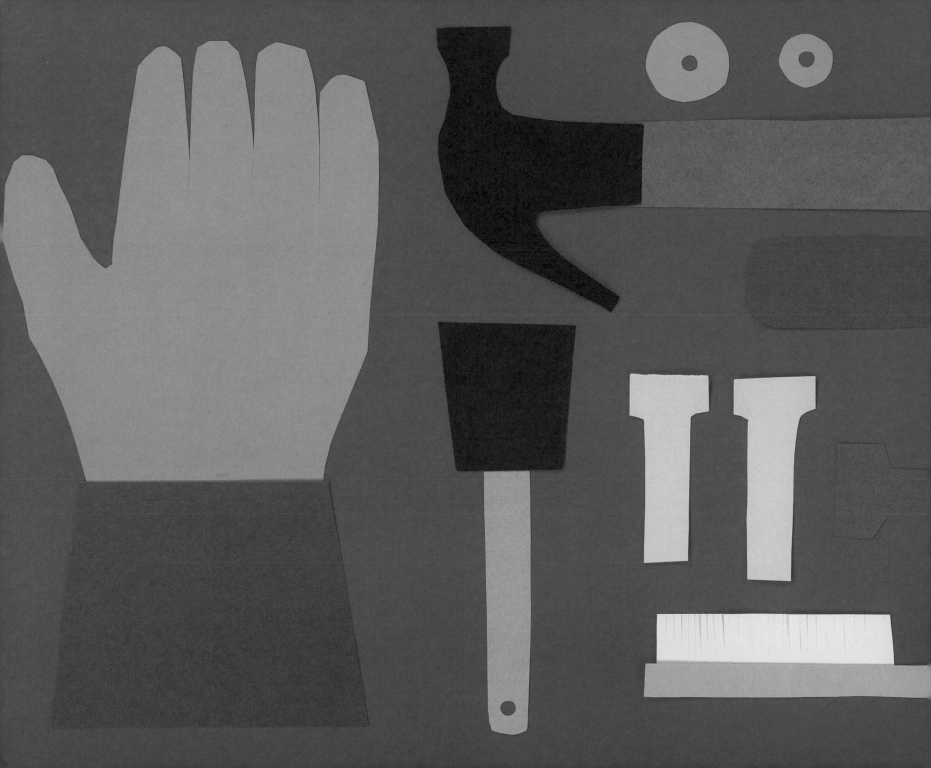

The workers used all kinds of tools in their work, and tried not to drop them into the ocean. (If you drop a hammer or wrench from a bridge hundreds of feet above the ocean, you're pretty much out of luck.)

EXTRA LARGE NAILS

Seeing the bridge rise was very exciting to the people of San Francisco and the Bay Area.

We should stop here and mention that today, San Francisco is a city of about 800,000. It is one of the more unusual cities in the world, given that it's built on and around 49 hills, some of them as high as 928 feet. Have you been to San Francisco? Some of these things you have to see to believe. It is a strange place.

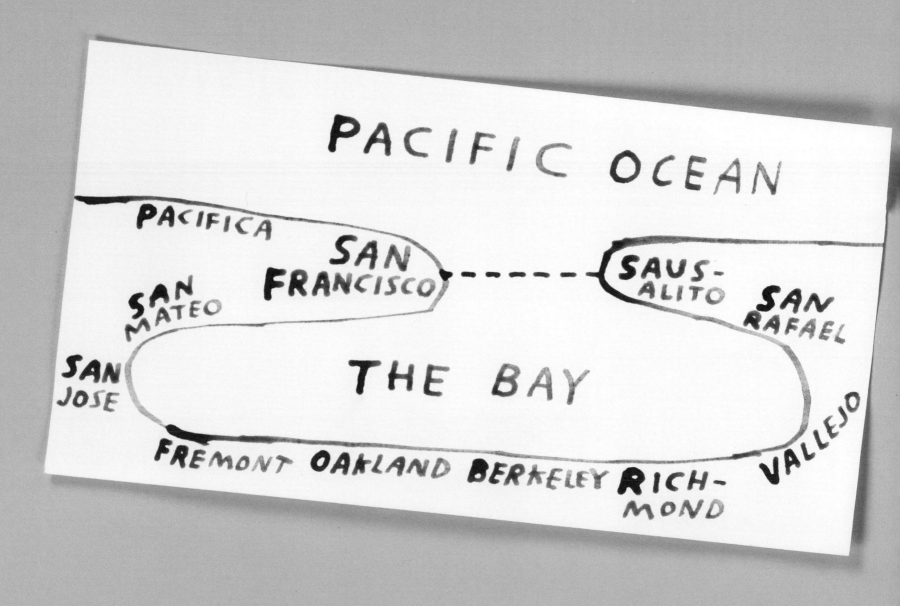

San Francisco is one of many dozens of cities and towns built around the Bay. Together, these cities and towns make up a region known as the Bay Area. The Bay it's named for is the one that leads to the Pacific Ocean.

And this bay leads to the Pacific Ocean through the Golden Gate. Remember that? And the Golden Gate was where they were building this bridge.

And it was going up just fine. They estimated that it would take four years to build it, with thousands of workers working on it.

But there was one thing that had not been decided. They had not decided what color to make the bridge. Isn't that a strange thing, that a very large group of adults would undertake a project of this size, and not have a color picked out?

But that's how it sometimes is. In this case, everyone decided that by the time the bridge was finished, they would have the color part figured out.

So they kept building it.

First there were the cables.

No. Wait. First there were the towers.

Of course the towers were first. And they were
astonishing to all.

When the towers were finished, it was a day
of great jubilation. This thing that had not
been there before was now there. The tops of
the towers were 746 feet above the water level.
Sometimes the things humans make baffle
even the humans who make them.

While the bridge was being finished,
though, people were still debating the
color. And the debate over the color
brought forth some very interesting ideas.

The Navy thought it
should be yellow and
black. No kidding. They
did. The Navy thought the
bridge would be safer that
way, so ships and planes
could easily see it.

The Army had a stranger idea: How about red
and white stripes? they said. This is true.
This is a factual book.

The Army wanted it to look like a candy cane for
the same reason the Navy wanted it to look like
a tiger with jaundice: so that it would be easily
seen by planes and ships.

But most people thought these were
not such great ideas. Most people
thought the sensible choice would
be one of the following:

WHITE

GRAY

These were the colors of most large human-made things. Most buildings were gray or black. Monuments and towers were usually white. And almost all bridges were gray. Gray was a serious color. Gray was practical. Gray was dignified. Who could object to gray?

A person named Irving could. And he did.

Irving Morrow had been watching the bridge rise.
He often rode on a ferry out near the bridge, and he
loved seeing the towers rise high above the water.
At that time, of course, the towers were orange.

The steelworkers who had created the bridge in its many pieces had done something before they sent the pieces of the bridge onto the railcars, then the boats, down the coast and through the canal and up the other coast: they had coated the pieces of steel in a kind of paint that prevented them from rusting.

They used this paint all the time. In fact, most of the steel they made and delivered came coated in this same paint. The color of this paint was a certain reddish orange.

NO FRILLS
ANTI-RUST
PAINT

When Irving Morrow was on the ferry one day, he watched this orange steel being assembled, and he had a thought. He thought that this color was beautiful.

And when Irving was asked what color he thought the bridge should be, he said, Why not leave it this color? And people said, What? And they said, Huh? And they said, Irving, you are nuts. No bridge had ever been orange. Who had ever heard of an orange bridge? No one had, because no bridge had ever been this color. This is true: no bridge in known human history had ever been orange.

And for a good portion of the human race, because something has not already been, that is a good reason to fear it coming to be.

But as the debate continued about the color of the bridge, an interesting thing happened. Other people noticed the same thing Irving had noticed: that this accidental orange somehow looked right.

A woman named Ada Clement noticed.

A man named
Beniamino Bufano
noticed.

And as the bridge continued to rise, and
more and more people saw the orange
steel against the green hills, above the blue
water, below the blue-and-white sky, they
said, For some reason, that looks right.

But still. No bridge had
ever been orange. Orange
was silly. So most of those
involved figured the bridge
would be gray. Gray was
serious. Gray was safe.

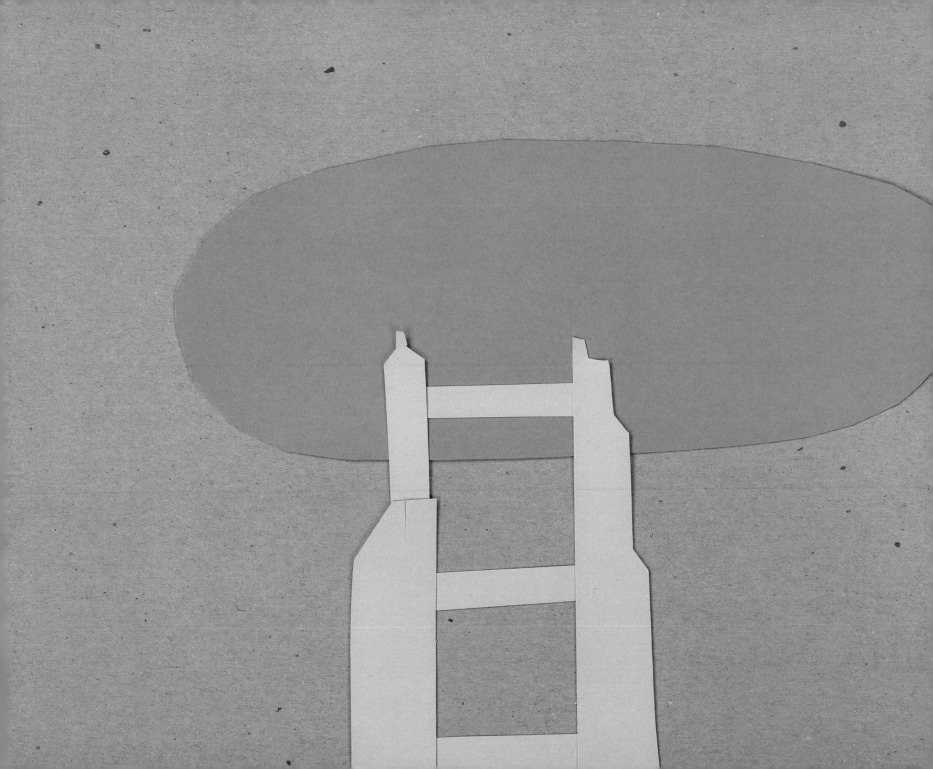

As they got closer to being finished with the bridge, though, and closer to painting it gray, Irving Morrow, who was a quiet man, who was a shy man, who was no fancy man with lots of power, began to get loud.

He wrote letters about the orange bridge.
He collected letters from others who believed an
orange bridge was the right thing. And his letters
became louder. And more insistent. He would
have to see this bridge every day for the
rest of his life. He did not want a
gray bridge.

This bridge, he told everyone, will not be gray. This bridge will not be gray.

And others began to echo him.

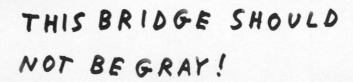

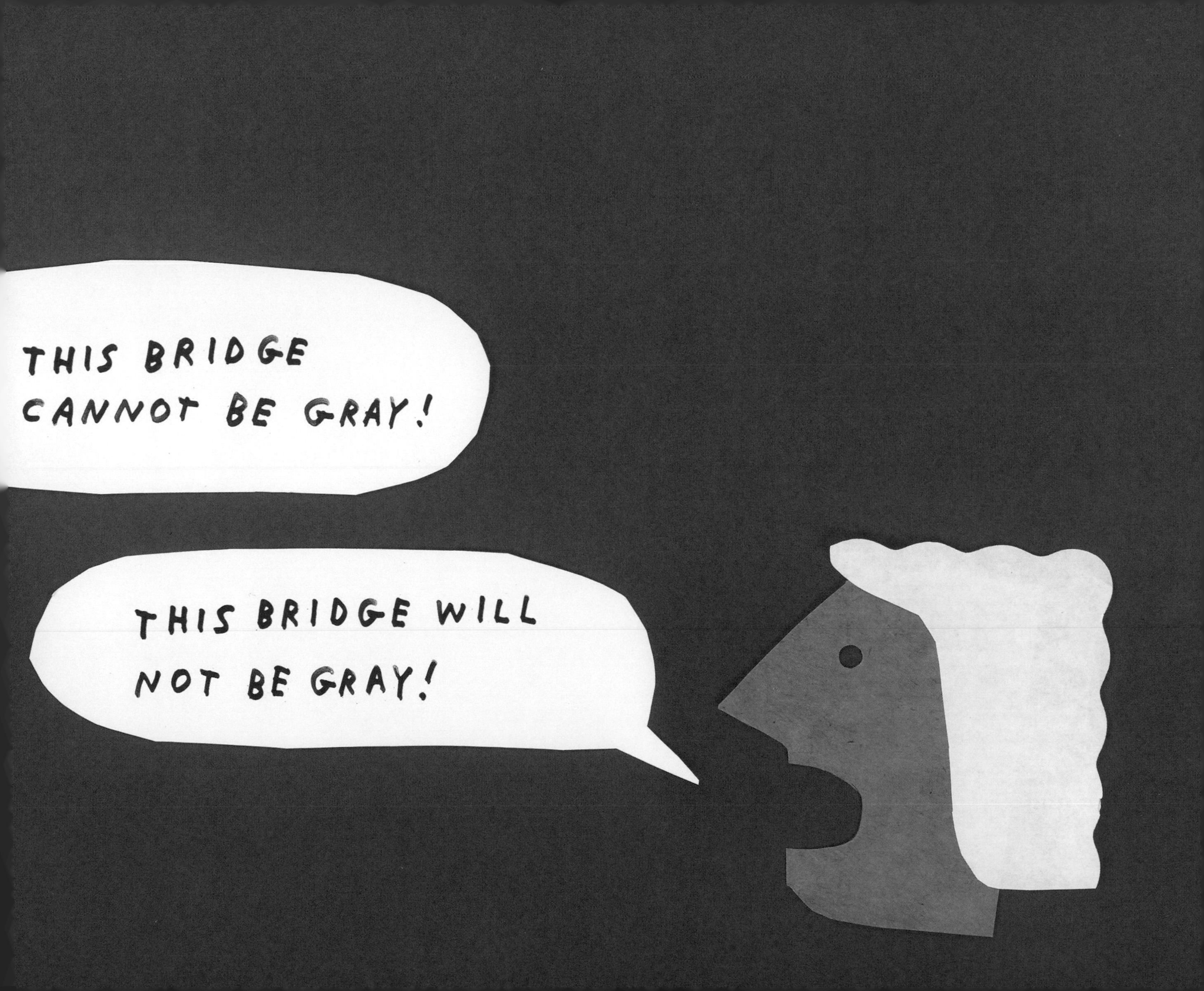
THIS BRIDGE CANNOT BE GRAY!
THIS BRIDGE WILL NOT BE GRAY!

Finally, the powers that be decided to try it.
And after some time they agreed with Irving that
though it was strange, and unprecedented, and
bold, the orange was the right color.

And so it was.

And so it stood.

And still stands today.

You know what they call the color of the bridge? It has an official name: International Orange.

But because the winds and fog and salt water in the Bay are harsh, the bridge needs to be repainted year-round. On any given day, painters are repainting some part of the bridge. They use 10,000 gallons of paint a year.

It is crazy that people repaint a bridge all year. It is crazy that people repaint an orange bridge all year with all that paint. But people love to paint it, and people love to look at it. The Golden Gate Bridge, which is orange, is the best-known and best-loved bridge in the world.

It is best-known because it is bold and courageous and unusual and even strange. It is best-loved because it is bold and courageous and unusual and even strange. And it is all these things because Irving Morrow, and thousands of others said:

THIS BRIDGE   WILL

The End

McSWEENEY'S

SAN FRANCISCO

Book design by Dan McKinley.

This book was produced with the help of Lea Simonds and Dylan Simonds.

Manufactured in China
ISBN 978-1-940450-47-6
First edition

2 4 6 8 10 9 7 5 3 1

www.mcsweeneys.net